The Greatest of These is Love

Clare Heather

BookLeaf
Publishing

India | USA | UK

Presentation by *BookLeaf Publishing*

Web: www.bookleafpub.com

E-mail: info@bookleafpub.com

ISBN : 9789357447331

First edition 2021

DEDICATION

Dedicated to anyone who has found freedom, hope, faith and healing whilst in the darkness.

I hope you find encouragement.

ACKNOWLEDGEMENT

Thank you to my God, the 3 in 1, for He is greater than all of my sufferings, and inspired me to write these poems.

Thank you to my friends and family for your love and support through my life.

Thank you to all of the teachers and everyone else in my communities, who ever believed in me and supported me in my creative endeavours.

Thank you to you reader for taking a chance on a little book of poems, I hope it is enjoyable and encouraging to you.

PREFACE

A Spiritual tale,
to inspire those that choose it.
One hopes it won't fail.

The Fall

They did not realise,
what they had done for a taste.
The Serpent tongue lies.

Ode to Anxiety

Old companion dear, I never cared for thee.
I know not where you came from or why you
came at all,
it seems your only purpose was to laugh and
watch me fall.

I hadn't known your name; it was anxiety.
You always found it easiest to make me feel so
small,
I didn't know I'd miss you until I couldn't hear
your call.

Now I never really liked you,
This much we know is true.
But I got used to your presence,
all the pain and all the hurt you caused.
You come and go now, changing hue,
guess you didn't like it when I was made anew.

The Plague

3

It's not the body,
but the mind that is the plague.
We need mental health.

The Greatest of These is Love

Many good things come from heav'n above,
of things I hold dear, this faith, love and hope.
But, the greatest of these is love.

The good news is brought by a faithful dove,
that there is more to life than just to cope.
Many good things come from heav'n above.

Despite the light, I feel the darkness shove.
I look to other things to broaden my scope,
the greatest of these is love.

There are so many things I must let go of,
I must remember this and choose not to mope,
many good things come from heav'n above.

My soul is sheathed like a hand in a glove.
His words are slippery to the dark like soap,
the greatest of these is love.

I need not reach for the hanging man's rope,

for through my faith in you, I have found my
hope.
Many good things come from heav'n above,
but, the greatest of these is love.

The Sculptor

His hands move deftly through the day,
his heart aglow with pride and love.
For all things beheld in his sight,
seem to be sent from the heavens above.

Before I came into being,
it was the sculptor alone that loved me.
Now I am alive and these eyes, they are seeing,
the world as he made it, the way it should be.

So, to this man I am grateful,
this vessel for me he has made.
How could I ever be hateful?
When beauty like ours can't be weighed.

Flowers

Now, I dream of roaming fields of flowers,
A small trail forms behind me, and traces.
To lie beneath bright canopies for hours,
I find so much beauty in these places.

Life can feel dark, lonely and frightening.
These flowers I conjure in my mind's eye,
begin to start my bleak world brightening,
then my world seems more wonderful to me.

But the world was never wholly that bleak,
it was my mind that cast shadows in it.
The illness did seem to make my heart weak,
in these times, with the flowers I would sit.

Now, the dark and the illness frights me not,
for these flowers I dream, I love a lot.

Just Casper

There once was a boy called "jee Casper".
He grew up in a place called Wee Jasper.
He had tan skin,
the air was thin,
and that's why he had asthma.

His parents struggled with the bills.
They said "it's alright we can afford your pills,"
they couldn't though.
He died in the snow
One winter in those rolling hills.

The funeral was in that town.
The guests told the parents not to frown,
they said, "he no longer needs those pills."
"He's forever in these rolling hills."
And there they laid him down.

There is a place called Wee Jasper.
Once home to a sick boy with asthma,
he has pale skin,
under the air that's thin,
and his grave stone reads just 'Casper'.

The Rain

The drops fall slow first.
The clouds weep powerfully,
my sorrows drowned out.

Warfare

We are at war,
what can I do?
The world is at war,
how could I help you?

Learn to build a foundation,
an armour to keep you strong.
Rely on these in every situation,
they've been inside you all along.

Truth like the belt that protects,
righteousness guards your heart,
peace brought by the Gospel,
guiding your feet is its part.

Prayer our attack, our defence and our help,
Faith is the shield.
Salvation, the helmet that defends the mind.
Spirit, His Word our weapon, the sword we
wield.

We are at war,
so stand firm.
The world is at war,

do everything, to stand.

Hope

When the dark comes,
and blackness is all I see.
There is light as small as a pin.
It begins to grows as I grow,
it is the light of hope within.

Recovering

Breathe.
Breathe.
Breathe.
You're doing good. Breathe.
Take your time. You're doing good. Breathe
Just stand up. Take your time. You're doing
good. Breathe.
I have to do this. Just stand up. Take your time.
You're doing good. Breathe.
I have to do this. Just stand up. Take your time.
You're doing good. Breathe.
I have to do this. Take your time. You're doing
good. Breathe.
I have to do this. You're doing good. Breathe.
I have to do this. Breathe.
I have to do this.
I have to do this.
I have to do this.

Mustard Seeds

From a seed so slight,
faith that small will also grow
in to trees so strong.

The Theatre

The atmosphere is buzzing,
voices murmur and exclaim.
Papers sound as seats are taken.
Excitement feels the same .

My breath catches. The lights they dim.
His arms, they raise.
My heart swells, when those first notes sound.
The curtain opens.
With tears in my eyes.

The show begins.

Moon and Stars

16

As I walk I drift into thoughts and dreams,
in the night's great cloak, the stars are the seams.
The moon, night's changing heart.
Each little light plays its part,
The moon and stars are night's beauty, it seems.

Sonnet of Peace

I desire to find true, authentic peace,
for far too long I have been shroud in fear.
Many others pray for their pain to cease,
they pray for something to make it all clear.

The world in all of its broken desires,
seem to seek their peace where it cannot thrive.
We watch and don't act as we see the fires.
All seems too bleak for our faith to survive.

But hope is not gone and our faith stays strong,
for in you we find the peace we long for.
Is it not true, we've had it all along?
We can have peace amongst these flames of war.

I need not, to seek this true peace for me,
just share what I know of the peace I see.

To Be Loved

Not always felt,
but always present.
I have finally accepted it.
The knowing, and the feeling
of being loved.

Seeking

Listen to what it is that I say,
Do you remember when you learnt?
What you did, that fateful day?
Throwing your problems on the fire and
watching as they burnt
And all that was left was a pile of ash, tall and
grey.

They didn't like when you changed your heart,
the thing that now you sought,
They didn't like to see you conquering your
fears, they didn't like your growth.
They didn't much like at all that you were brave,
and that they weren't,
they didn't like that you turned around and
returned what you had bought.

For once, you stood in shadows; fear controlled
your life,
But now you've started seeking the thing that
ends your strife.
The thing you seek, when found won't break,
and rarely bend
When it's found, you mustn't fear the price you
need not pay.

Your time for fear is over now, put away that
rusty knife
The thing you seek is forever and will never
have an end.

The thing you seek is freedom. Freedom, peace
and joy.

Clouds

The ever changing,
dream filled, beauties of the sky.
I long to join you.

One Step

One step at a time is all I can manage.
My arms stretched forward,
reaching, for my salvation.

I become distracted.
My doubts and fears like waves,
crash into me and drag me down.

I panic. I can't breathe. Drowning.
I'm drowning, sinking under the turmoil.
The darkness returning. Surely this is my end.

I feel a tug at my hand, I am too weak.
I try to fight the waves but I'm not strong
enough.
I feel it again and look up into the mess, at the
hand in mine.

I am lifted from the water.
I look into His face and feel peace again,
I take one step.
I take another.

The Princess and The Horse

A plain girl born of middle stock,
thought nothing much about her lot.
She wished her mind was under lock,
you see her thoughts had start to rot.

A darkness shook her very core,
a whisper yelled into her mind.
Her body fits, her hands some more.
The fear of death is all she'll find.

Then she's awake.
Her chest in pain.
Strength she tries to make,
to make in vain.

With trees she spoke when she was out.
Another roamed between the fir.
The forests never brought her doubt,
and then the man did find her.

The man was known this much was true,
though she never thought she'd meet him.

The man, the King knew what to do,
to help the girl escape the grim.

A crown he held between his hands,
symbolic of peace she was seeking.
'My daughter, we had other plans."
Of her life she knew he was speaking.

The two in comfort walked side by side,
the road then split. A choice of path.
He went left and the girl too tried,
to no avail, for her heart in wrath.

The anger swelled within her,
destined for one road.
A path of darkness as it were,
alone again, this load.

In mourning joy, the girl did fall.
Her breathing laboured more.
Her heart did race, she tried to call,
her voice was gone and sore.

After what felt like forever,
there stood by her side,
a beast so clever.
Here a horse to ride.

"Hullo, dear child!"

The horse did cry.
The girl did see it's friendly smile.
It waited for her tears to dry.

When she had gained her energy.
The horse was patiently waiting,
"You mustn't judge your lethargy.
You are strong, it's the truth that I'm stating."

The girl shook her head in doubt,
"Which of these ways are we going?"
The horse had asked, she pointed the track out.
"No, there's bad things in there growing."

She told the horse, about the King.
Sorrow welled within her chest again,
"Don't you fret child, the birds still sing."
she listened and plaited the horses mane.

"You know, dear girl, you can choose to go left,
the crown you've got there on your head.
It wasn't put there to leave you bereft,
it's the way you can follow where he's tread."

The girl reached up and touched the crown,
she'd forgotten it was there.
She looked at the paths, then to the horse with a
frown.
She wasn't sure she could follow with the mare.

"Fear not, fair child I was sent to you,
by the King who loves you, dear.
He wouldn't take a friend from you.
How much you'd gone through with your fear?"

The Princess wrapped her arms around its neck,
and the horse returned the hug.
"Lets go my friend, down the better trek."
The Princess sat on the rug.

Together they rode down the left track,
the light was brighter here.
A weight had lifted from her back.
The Princess had nothing to fear.

Limits

I've often been told,
The sky is the limit.
It makes me feel bold,
I believe it no less.
For the sky we behold,
Well it is limitless.